COLIN POWELL

ALSO BY ELAINE LANDAU

ALZHEIMER'S DISEASE

BLACK MARKET ADOPTION
AND THE SALE OF CHILDREN

COWBOYS

DYSLEXIA

INTERESTING INVERTEBRATES:
A Look at Some Animals Without Backbones

JUPITER

LYME DISEASE

MARS

NAZI WAR CRIMINALS

NEPTUNE

ROBERT FULTON

SATURN

THE SIOUX

SURROGATE MOTHERS

TROPICAL RAIN FORESTS AROUND THE WORLD

WE HAVE AIDS

WE SURVIVED THE HOLOCAUST

WILDFLOWERS AROUND THE WORLD

COLIN POWELL

FOUR-STAR GENERAL

BY ELAINE LANDAU

A FIRST BOOK

FRANKLIN WATTS

NEW YORK ★ LONDON ★ TORONTO ★ SYDNEY ★ 1991

Cover photograph copyright © :   Photri

Photographs copyright © : New York Public Library, Picture
Collection: pp. 8, 11; AP/Wide World Photos: pp. 13, 14, 23, 28, 29,
30, 36, 40, 43, 46, 48, 50, 51, 53; UPI/Bettmann Newsphotos: pp. 16,
31; Office of the Chairman of the Joint Chiefs of Staff: pp. 34, 45, 54
(all Robert D. Ward), 17, 21, 25, 38.

Library of Congress Cataloging–in–Publication Data

Landau, Elaine.
Colin Powell: four-star general / by Elaine Landau.
p.   cm. -- (A first book)
Includes bibliographical references and index.
Summary: Examines the life and career of General Colin L.
Powell, the first black chairman of the Joint Chiefs of Staff.
ISBN 0-531-20143-0
1. Powell, Colin L.--Juvenile literature.   2. Generals--United
States--Biography--Juvenile literature.   3. Afro-American
generals--Biography--Juvenile literature.   4. United
States.   Army--Biography--Juvenile literature.   [1. Powell,
Colin L.   2. Generals.   3. Afro-Americans--Biography.]
I. Title.
II. Series.
E840.5.P68L36   1991
355′.0092--dc20
[B]   91-12860 CIP AC

CONTENTS

FOR LINDA—
a librarian, community organizer,
and mother of two

COLIN POWELL

Colin Powell was born in a New York City neighborhood called Harlem. This overview of New York City shows the high-rise community and the Harlem River bordering the area.

CHAPTER ONE

IN THE BEGINNING

It was nearly spring in New York City's Harlem community. Luther Powell and his wife Maud Ariel (McKoy) Powell eagerly awaited the birth of their second child. They already had a young daughter. The African American couple had come to the United States over twenty years ago from the Caribbean island of Jamaica. They were hardworking, industrious people. Luther was a shipping clerk in New York City's garment center—a clothing manufacturing district. His wife also worked there as a seamstress.

On April 5, 1937, Maud Ariel gave birth to a son, whom they named Colin Luther. The Powell children profited from growing up in a strong loving family. The close bond they shared helped Colin to develop a firm sense of self-confidence. He was taught to believe in himself and not readily accept the limitations others might set for him.

Although Maud and Luther had not completed high school, they often stressed the importance of education to their children. At a young age, Colin knew that learning was the route to success, and that success was only achieved through hard work. It was important to Colin to do well. He was part of a proud family, and it was up to him to uphold that tradition.

While Colin was still a young boy, his family moved from Harlem to the Bronx, a borough of New York City. They lived in a low-rent area, and their apartment building was hardly luxurious. As a child, Colin attended local public schools. At first, he was not an outstanding scholar. While a fifth grader at elementary school P.S. 39, he was put in a class for slow students. But Colin refused to give up. He knew that if he kept trying, he would succeed.

Later on, Colin earned average grades at Morris High School in the Bronx. He continued his education at the City College of New York, where he enrolled in the school's

Powell spent his boyhood in the busy New York City borough of the Bronx. The land had once been a large farm owned by a Danish immigrant named Jonas Bronck. Known as "The Bronck's Farm," the name stuck long after the farm had disappeared.

★ ★ ★ ★

Reserve Officers Training Corps (ROTC). The ROTC program trains college students to become officers in the armed services. At ROTC, Colin Powell began to earn A's.

As was true of many intelligent, ambitious, young African Americans in the 1950s, Colin Powell thought seriously about an Army career. Unfortunately, racial prejudice and discrimination limited opportunities for African Americans in many other fields. At one time, African Americans had been given more than their share of dirty and dangerous jobs in the U.S. Army too. But in 1948, President Harry Truman stopped the practice of grouping military units according to race. In an integrated army, soldiers were expected to share the same responsibilities and promotion possibilities regardless of color.

By the 1950s, opportunities for African Americans in the military were better than in civilian life. The Army was known to both actively recruit and advance minority group members, although some discrimination still existed. An African American could rise to the rank of admiral or general if he were qualified. At the same time, becoming president of a large corporation was a less likely goal. The promise of steady employment, good health and education benefits, and a chance to compete fairly drew young African Americans to the service.

Colin Powell made an excellent choice in enrolling in ROTC. He proved to be well-suited to military discipline, and while in training, demonstrated outstanding leadership

Colin Powell had been an outstanding ROTC member while at the City College of New York. Here City College ROTC students march in the annual President's Day Review.

*Prior to the army's desegregation,
a World War II African American
machine-gun crew sets up its equipment.*

qualities. His classmates remember that Powell motivated others around him. In 1958, he graduated from college at the top of his ROTC class. At the time, Colin Powell had been promoted to cadet colonel—the corps' highest rank.

Following graduation, Powell became a second lieutenant in the United States Army. Standing over six feet tall, the handsome young officer had a proud military bearing. In 1962, he went on a blind date with a young woman named Alma Vivian Johnson. She was the daughter of a well-known and respected high school principal. Colin and Alma fell in love and were married that August.

The couple wasn't married for very long before Powell was called off to war. In 1963, he left his young bride to fight for his country in Vietnam. Powell's wife gave birth to their first child, Michael, while Powell was in Vietnam. The baby was nearly two weeks old before Powell learned he was a father. At the time, Powell was among 16,000 U.S. military advisers sent to southeast Asia by then-President John F. Kennedy. He was assigned to a unit patrolling the border area between Vietnam and Laos.

These soldiers often had to dodge enemy bullets as well as different types of mines and traps. One day in 1963, while marching through a damp rice paddy, Colin Powell stepped on a device known as a Punji-stick trap. As his foot touched the trap, a sharpened stake shot through the bottom. After his injury, Powell received a Purple Heart. Later that year, the young officer was awarded a Bronze Medal.

*American soldiers patrol the Laotian border
during the Vietnam War just as Colin Powell
did when he was stationed there.*

*As shown here, African Americans
risked their lives for their country,
but were discriminated against at home.*

Colin Powell distinguished himself on many occasions in Vietnam. Even as a young soldier, he had impressed his superiors. One of Powell's early battalion commanders described him as "wise beyond his years." Powell performed well on all his assignments. He was known for his ability to think and plan ahead.

Powell's bravery in helping fellow soldiers was evident as well. Even after he was injured in a helicopter crash, he continued to rescue other soldiers from the burning chopper. This heroic feat earned him a soldier's medal. Yet, unfortunately, even African American heroes were not shielded from racial discrimination.

Colin Powell bravely served his country. But in the early 1960s, some southern restaurants still refused to serve him. When he was stationed at Fort Benning, Georgia, Powell went to the nearby town of Columbus to look for a place for his family to live. While he was house hunting, he stopped at a luncheonette for something to eat. The waitress asked him if he was an African student. When Powell said no, she asked him if he was Puerto Rican. After Powell said no a second time, she asked if he was a Negro. Powell replied, "That's right." Then the waitress told him: "Well, I can't bring out a hamburger. You'll have to go to the back door."

CHAPTER TWO

THE LADDER OF SUCCESS

No matter how much he accomplished, Colin Powell continued to try to improve himself. After returning from a second tour of duty in Vietnam, he decided to further his education. He enrolled at George Washington University in Washington, D.C. By 1971, he had earned a master's degree in business administration.

The following year, Powell was promoted to the rank of major. But 1972 marked a turning point in the military officer's career for another reason. That year, Colin Powell was selected from over 1,500 candidates to be one of seventeen White House Fellows. This was an extremely sought-after political opportunity. White House Fellows were promising individuals who were provided with the necessary experience and training for high government positions.

While at the White House, Powell was an assistant to the

deputy director of the Office of Management and Budget. Those who worked with Powell were impressed with his performance. He was intelligent and efficient, and an outstanding decision-maker. Within a short time, his superiors knew he would be back at the White House some day. Colin Powell would be a valuable asset to any administration.

The next few years were busy ones for Powell. He took on new duties and responsibilities as he rose through the Army's ranks. In 1973, he was sent to Korea, where he served as a battalion commander. He was called back to work in the Pentagon the following year. Powell then enrolled in the National War College in 1975. He had only completed seven months of a nine-month course when he was assigned command of the Second Brigade of the 101 Airborne Division at Fort Campbell, Kentucky. But even though he had to leave the college, Powell continued to study on his own. In 1976, he graduated with honors.

During President Jimmy Carter's administration (1976–1980), Colin Powell was promoted to major general. He also held two important positions, serving first as senior military assistant to the deputy defense secretary and then as executive assistant to the Secretary of Energy.

Following these political positions, Powell returned to what he liked best—working with the troops. He was serving as deputy commander at Fort Leavenworth in Kansas in 1982 when Secretary of Defense Caspar Weinberger asked him to return to Washington. Weinberger needed a senior

*Although Powell did well in both political
and military work, he especially
liked working with the troops.*

military assistant, and he remembered the bright, capable, White House Fellow he had worked with nearly a decade earlier.

Weinberger wanted Powell for the job, but the major general had some serious doubts about taking the position. Working in the field meant a great deal to Colin Powell. Yet his many Washington assignments had taken him away from that. Now that he was back with his men, he wasn't sure he wanted to return to a desk job. However, Weinberger was equally determined not to give up on having Powell work for him. He finally convinced the major general to "come aboard."

It proved to be the right decision for both Powell and the nation. Before long, Weinberger and Powell were known around Washington as a top Pentagon team. Their work took the pair to over thirty-five countries. Weinberger tackled tough assignments with Powell at his side. He often spoke highly of Powell. Weinberger knew he had a knowledgable assistant whom he could depend on.

Colin Powell was dedicated to accomplishing the tasks at hand. He usually arrived at his office at 6:30 in the morning and didn't leave until 7 in the evening. He was thought of as someone who worked well within the system. Powell easily grasped major policy issues. And in a low-keyed, professional manner, he often accomplished what others were unable to do. Pentagon insiders were comfortable around

*Powell meets with senators Howard Baker
and Robert Dole. Powell was known for his
ability to get the job done.*

Powell. As Weinberger's assistant, Powell came to be thought of as a sort of "junior" Secretary of Defense.

In 1986, Powell was once again given a chance to work directly with soldiers. He eagerly accepted the post of commanding general of the Fifth Corps. The new assignment put him in charge of 72,000 troops stationed in West Germany. Powell thoroughly enjoyed his new job. But before long, he received another telephone call from Washington that would once again change the direction of his career.

This time, Frank Carlucci, President Ronald Reagan's new national security adviser, asked Powell to be his deputy (second in command) at the White House. Although it was a wonderful opportunity, Powell graciously declined. He had already spent a good part of his career in policy-making positions. Now he intended to continue as a commanding general.

Carlucci called Powell a number of times, urging him to change his mind; still the major general refused. In fact, Powell remained firm in his decision until President Reagan himself called to emphasize just how much Powell was wanted in Washington.

At that point, Colin Powell agreed to return to the capital to begin work in January 1987. When asked what changed his mind, he said that as a United States serviceman he was happy to serve his country wherever he was needed most. In

*Colin Powell was extremely helpful in improving
a number of military procedures while serving in
President Ronald Reagan's administration.*

his new position, Powell helped to redesign the National Security Council. The council is a board composed of various department heads that advise the president on defense and foreign policy matters. Powell also improved the existing methods for keeping the president informed.

Powell worked extremely well with his new superior, Frank Carlucci. The men had similar views on important issues. One of the national security adviser's daily tasks is to brief the president on current matters. Carlucci often sent Powell in by himself to speak to President Reagan. He wanted the president to share the trust and confidence he, Carlucci, had in Powell. President Reagan was quite impressed with Carlucci's assistant. Before long, people in Washington were saying that the deputy national security adviser was sure to go far.

They were right. When, on November 5, 1987, President Reagan promoted Frank Carlucci to a higher position, Powell moved up as well. He became Reagan's national security adviser. In his new position, Powell was one of the most powerful African Americans ever to serve in government. Each day he met with both the secretary of state and the defense secretary. Then Powell joined the president in the White House Oval Office to inform him of important recent developments. As national security adviser, Powell could reach the president twenty-four hours a day by telephone.

As in the past, Powell performed the tasks assigned him with ease and precision. He played a vital role in planning a series of superpower summits between President Reagan and Soviet President Mikhail Gorbachev. Colin Powell even received the Distinguished Service Award for his work on a U.S.–Soviet arms agreement and a Moscow summit. He was also a key figure in helping to shape United States foreign policy. Powell worked closely with the president when U.S. forces were sent into Grenada and Panama.

As Colin Powell advanced in his career, he never made race an issue. While serving as an army general, he once said in a television interview, "What my color is is somebody else's problem, not mine. People will say, 'You're a terrific black general.' [But] I'm [just] trying to be the best general I can be."[1] To a great extent, Powell's achievements in various areas tended to overshadow the fact that he is also a member of a minority group. In countless situations, he accomplished more than most of his contemporaries, regardless of race.

Colin Powell wants to be judged by his ability rather than his skin color, but that doesn't mean he doesn't care deeply about his people. He is well aware of the sacrifices made by other African Americans who paved the way for his own success. Powell described his feelings in an address to the women's auxiliary of one of Washington's oldest African American patriotic organizations this way:

*In Moscow, Powell, Secretary of State George Shultz,
and others plan upcoming talks with Soviet President
Mikhail Gorbachev, who sits across the table from them.*

*Powell congratulates a soldier
who took part in the United States
assault on Panamanian defense forces.*

*Colin Powell appreciated the sacrifices made by
African American soldiers throughout America's history.
Here African Americans serving in World War II practice
first-aid techniques as they prepare for combat duty.*

An African American soldier wounded in Vietnam is assisted by medics.

When I came along in 1958, I was able to capture all of what was done before me by men in segregated units denied the opportunity to advance. . . . It's different now, but we still have a long way to go. We should be grateful for what the men and women have done before. We cannot let the torch drop.[2]

CHAPTER THREE

TOP GUN

As President Reagan's term drew to a close, Colin Powell looked forward to leaving Washington to begin working again directly with the troops. He had been offered both a promotion and an exciting new post. President Reagan raised Powell to the rank of a four-star general. There are just ten full (four-star) generals in the entire United States Armed Forces. Powell is the only African American among them. Powell also took over the U.S. Forces Command at Fort McPherson, Georgia. This meant that he would head all army ground forces in the continental United States.

But even more exciting challenges lay ahead. In August 1989, President George Bush nominated Powell as Joint Chiefs of Staff (JCS) chairman. The Joint Chiefs of Staff is the most important military advisory group in the nation. It includes the chiefs of staff for the army and air force, the chief of naval operations, and the commandant of the

The chairman meets with members of the Joint Chiefs of Staff.

Marine Corps, as well as other members. The chairman of the Joint Chiefs of Staff outranks all other military officials and presides at meetings.

The Joint Chiefs of Staff chairman is also the principal military adviser to the president and the secretary of defense. He must keep them informed of the troops' well-being and readiness for combat. He must also advise them on the advantages and disadvantages of using U.S. armed forces in various situations.

Although the Joint Chiefs of Staff chairman is appointed by the president, he must be approved by the United States Senate. If approved, Colin Powell would be the first African American to hold the nation's top military post. At fifty-two years of age, he would also be the youngest JCS chairman in the history of the country.

In nominating Colin Powell for the job, President Bush passed over at least thirty other generals. While Powell lacked the lengthy combat experience of some, he had other important assets. He was a natural leader who was just as comfortable speaking to foreign heads of state as to infantry soldiers. He was also a top-level manager, often demonstrating both strength and flexibility in crisis situations. And at a time when many Americans were questioning the ethics of government officials, Colin Powell was known for his high moral standards.

Senate approval of Powell came quickly and easily.

*General Powell is greeted, from right to left,
by Senate Arms Services Committee members senators
Daniel Moynihan of New York, John Warner of Virginia,
and Sam Nunn of Georgia.*

During the two-day Senate hearings, not a single objection was raised to his nomination. At the time, Senate committee chairman Sam Nunn told the press that the four-star general brings "tremendous . . . talent, insight, and experience to the post."[1]

Perhaps Powell's memories as a young soldier sent off to war would be especially valuable to him in his new position. He knew exactly what it was like to fight on the front lines. Maybe that is why, at his welcoming ceremony as Joint Chiefs of Staff chairman, Powell chose not to speak about the defense budget or international relations.

Instead, he talked about a painting of a church that hangs in the Pentagon. The church is empty except for the appearance of a single family. The mother, father, son, and daughter are praying at the altar rail. The father is in uniform and there is the feeling that this is the last time they will be praying together before he goes off to war.

It could be a painting of any American military family, including Colin Powell's. Powell always regarded his family as an important part of his life. Even after working long hours, he made certain he had time for them. Sometimes they would watch old movies together or talk animatedly as Powell worked at one of his favorite hobbies—fixing old Volvo cars.

Other than the son born while he was in Vietnam, Colin and Alma Powell have two daughters. Linda is an actress

Alma Powell looks on as her husband is sworn into office.

and her sister, Annemarie, is a student at the College of William and Mary, in Williamsburg, Virginia.

Their son, Michael, chose to follow in his father's footsteps and embark on an Army career. However, while serving as a first lieutenant in Germany, he was involved in a serious automobile accident. Michael was so badly injured that he needed over twenty pints of blood and had to remain in the hospital for nearly a year. Fortunately, he survived. But due to his injuries, an army career was no longer possible. He is now a student at Georgetown law school.

As both a soldier and a father, Colin Powell knows how devastating the death or injury of a military person can be to a family. Now as Joint Chiefs of Staff chairman, Powell will help determine exactly when and where United States combat troops will be used. Once the U.S. is involved in any type of armed struggle, some soldiers will undoubtedly die. Colin Powell faces the difficult task of balancing the troops' welfare against the country's needs.

In making the right choices, Powell stresses the importance of maintaining high standards. He has said, ''[We must be certain] that our armed forces . . . remain [strong] . . . that they always have what is needed to accomplish their mission . . . that they are never asked to respond to the call of an uncertain trumpet. . . . We owe them and the nation, and the world no less.''[2]

Wartime decisions may not always be easy for any U.S.

general to make. But many feel both our soldiers and country will do well with Colin Powell in charge. A friend once described him as a "tough-as-nails military man" with "compassion and soul."

Powell poses with First Capt. Cadet Kristin Baker following a West Point graduation ceremony. Powell was the featured speaker at the graduation, and Baker the first woman brigade commander.

CHAPTER FOUR

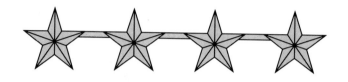

DESERT STORM—
AND BEYOND

When Colin Powell became Joint Chiefs of Staff chairman in October 1989, there was much for him to do. He was expected to argue in favor of the Pentagon's plan to spend billions of dollars on new weapons and programs. He also had to work with various military chiefs (army, navy, air force, etc.) to plan future arms-control agreements.

By the following summer, however, his attention shifted to a serious crisis in the Middle East. On August 2, 1990, Iraqi President Saddam Hussein invaded the small country of Kuwait. In response, United States soldiers, along with troops from other countries, were sent to the Persian Gulf region as a multinational force against Hussein. The main objective was to force the Iraqi president to withdraw from Kuwait. The multinational force also hoped to prevent him from invading Saudi Arabia.

The United States committed the largest number of

While in Saudi Arabia just prior to the outbreak of the Persian Gulf War, General Powell inspects U.S. equipment and provisions.

troops as well as the most money to this effort. Therefore, it had an important say in when an attack on Hussein's forces would occur and how extensive it might be if he didn't withdraw voluntarily. In developing a war plan, President Bush relied heavily on the advice of both Defense Secretary Dick Cheney and General Colin Powell. At first, Powell felt it might be best to continue economic sanctions against Iraq before using military force. However, Powell stressed that any attack, if it should come to that, should be massive and swift. As he explained it, "If you are going to commit the armed forces of the United States to a military operation that could involve conflict and loss of life, then do it right."[1]

In fact, just hours after Iraqi troops marched into Kuwait, Powell spoke to the president about a possible U.S. strategy. The plan he presented involved the greatest concentration of U.S. combat power since the Vietnam War. As Powell told a veterans' group he addressed, "No Iraqi leader should think for a moment that we don't have the will or ability to accomplish what might be required of us."[2]

General Powell was crucial in shaping U.S. military action in the Persian Gulf after Hussein's Kuwait invasion. "Don't count on easy ways," Powell warned the president. "You can't put a ship in the Gulf and lob shells and do anything."[3] Powell believes, in short, that if you want to be a superpower, you have to act like one. Just a symbolic show of strength might be mistaken for a sign of weakness. And that could result in a greater loss of life.

* * * *

44

*President Bush consults with General Powell
and top Department of Defense and National Security
advisers on Iraq's invasion of Kuwait.*

MAIN OPERATING BASES
DISPERSAL AIRFIELDS
SCUD LAUNCH AREAS

*The chairman of the Joint Chiefs of Staff points
to Iraqi air bases that had shown some activity
during the first few days of the Persian Gulf War.*

It was hoped that Saddam Hussein might leave Kuwait as he watched the massive troop buildup in Saudi Arabia. But when the Iraqi leader didn't budge, the first attacks against him were launched. On January 16, 1991, President Bush announced in Washington, "The liberation of Kuwait has begun." Wave after wave of warplanes streaked through the nighttime sky. The tremendous air offensive was aimed at Iraqi troops and military targets.

In addition, 500,000 U.S. soldiers were stationed in the Gulf. Colin Powell had a ready reply for those who felt the United States should not be involved in the Gulf conflict. He declared, "One of the fondest expressions around is that we can't be the world's policeman. But who gets called when someone suddenly needs a cop?"[4]

During the first six nights of the war, the four-star general slept on a couch in his office. He wanted to be nearby, to monitor events. In planning for victory, Powell said that the multinational force would first isolate the "brains of the operation." The next step would be to cut off Iraqi troops from food and ammunition supplies.

During the armed struggle, Powell kept in close touch with the troops. Wearing army fatigues while standing with his hands on his hips, Powell spoke casually with the servicemen and women. He thanked the troops for "bringing back a sense of pride to America."

He went on to say, "Wherever I go, people want to shake my hand and pat me on the back. But it's your hand

*General Powell and Secretary of Defense Dick Cheney
speak to members of the 354th Tactical Fighter Wing
from Myrtle Beach, South Carolina, at their air base
in Saudi Arabia. Notice the anti-tank
plane in the background.*

they want to shake and your back they want to pat." Powell promised that he would do his best to "get you back home to your loved ones."[5]

The four-star general stated, "We want to get this over as quickly as possible and in a way that leaves no doubt who won. And with a minimum of loss of life to our forces."[6] Adding a touch of humor, Powell left a short message for the Iraqi president on the casing of a 2,000-pound bomb to be dropped on Iraq. He wrote, "You didn't move it and now you'll lose it."[7] He signed the note, Colin Powell.

Although Powell believed that a strong show of force was necessary in the Gulf, he doesn't think any country should routinely rely on its military to settle disputes. At an international meeting of military heads from thirty-four countries, Powell described the armed forces' relationship to our Constitution as follows:

> *The U.S. Constitution is a remarkable document — and a demanding one for those of us who choose to make our career in the military. [The Constitution] looks at the military . . . as necessary but undesirable . . . useful in times of crisis and to be watched carefully at all other times.[8]*

Some people say our country has not had a general as outstanding as Colin Powell since President Dwight D. Eisenhower commanded World War II troops. There is even talk of Powell becoming vice president one day.

★ ★ ★ ★

General Powell sips Arab coffee with
General Norman Schwarzkopf on a visit to
Saudi Arabia to speak with field commanders
and soldiers during the Persian Gulf War.

Visiting with troops in Saudi Arabia,
General Powell jokingly autographs a
Saudi monetary note while leaning on
Air Force Sgt. Thaddeus Fernandez's head.

African American leader Jesse Jackson has described the four-star general as "presidential material." Although he has worked for Republican administrations, Powell hasn't declared himself yet as either a Republican or a Democrat. Therefore, he might be asked by either party to first run for vice president. However, General Powell's family claims he does not have any secret political desires. They stress that he is more concerned about his country than his personal advancement.

It is impossible to tell what the future holds. In the meantime, Colin Powell continues to do his best in his nation's military struggles. He is also concerned about the plight of African Americans at home. Despite his success, Powell has still experienced racial prejudice. As Deputy National Security Adviser for President Reagan, he was once sent to a commuter airlines terminal to pick up a VIP. Powell was the only person in the small terminal. Nevertheless, the airlines clerk on duty purposely ignored him. It wasn't until Powell introduced himself that the clerk realized that he had slighted one of the military's top generals.

Colin Powell has shown a special interest in African American youth. In spite of his busy schedule, he has tried to find time to speak to students. Powell feels it is important for young African Americans to have good role models. To that end, he has visited elementary schools, and junior and senior high school classes. Powell encourages those in his audience to make the most of their lives.

*Colin Powell and First Lady Barbara Bush
enjoy each other's company at a Washington, D.C.,
reception to honor President Bush's African American
appointees to his administration.*

When asked about the best route to success, General Powell wrote the following in a magazine for young African Americans:

There are no secrets to success; don't waste time looking for them. Success is the result of perfection, hard work, learning from failure, loyalty to those for whom you work, and persistence. You must be ready for opportunity when it comes.[9]

Opportunity came to Colin Powell and he took full advantage of it. He hopes that more opportunities will soon be available to other African Americans.

Colin Powell has shown a special interest in African American youth and frequently speaks before student and community groups.

SOURCE NOTES

CHAPTER 2

1. *Ebony*, July 1988, p. 140.
2. *Jet*, November 30, 1987, p. 16.

CHAPTER 3

1. *Jet*, October 9, 1989, p. 4.
2. *Jet*, October 23, 1989, p. 5.

CHAPTER 4

1. *Time*, November 12, 1990, p. 27.
2. *Newsweek*, September 3, 1990, p. 36.
3. *Ibid.*
4. *Life*, March 1991, p. 53.
5. *The Star Ledger*, February 11, 1991, p. 9.
6. *Ibid.*
7. *Ibid.*
8. *U.S. News & World Report*, February 4, 1991, p. 27.
9. *Ebony, op. cit.*, p. 146.

GLOSSARY

Battalion—a body of troops

Joint Chiefs of Staff—the United States's highest military advisory group; it includes chiefs of staff of the Army and Air Force, the chief of Naval operations, the Marine Corps's commandant, and a chairman and vice chairman

Multinational—involving more than one nation

Pentagon—the military establishment of the United States

Reserve Officers Training Corps (ROTC)—a program offered in schools and colleges that trains students to become officers in the United States armed services

Secretary of Defense—the head of the Department of Defense who is also a member of the president's cabinet

Secretary of Energy—the person who directs the Department of Energy and serves as the president's chief adviser on energy

Segregate—to separate according to race, social class, or some other trait

Summit—a meeting of heads of government

VIP—a very important person

FOR FURTHER READING

Adler, David. *Jackie Robinson: He Was The First*. New York: Holiday House, 1989.

———— *A Picture Book of Martin Luther King*. New York: Holiday House, 1989.

Graff, Stewart. *The Story of World War II*. New York: Dutton, 1978.

Haskins, James. *Count Your Way Through the Arab World*. Minneapolis, Minnesota: Carolrhoda Books, 1987.

Lawson, Don. *The War in Vietnam*. New York: Franklin Watts, 1981.

McKissack, Patricia C. *Jesse Jackson*. New York: Scholastic, 1989.

Messenger, Charles. *Combat Aircraft*. New York: Franklin Watts, 1984.

Petersen, David. *Submarines*. Chicago: Children's Press, 1984.

Pimlott, John. *The First World War*. New York: Franklin Watts, 1984.

Schneiderman, Ron. *The Picture Life of George Bush*. New York: Franklin Watts, 1989.

Sullivan, George. *Strange but True Stories of World War II*. New York: Walker, 1983.

Van Orden, M. D. *The Book of United States Navy Ships*. New York: Dodd Mead, 1985.

INDEX

★ ★ ★ ★

ABOUT THE AUTHOR

ELAINE LANDAU received her B.A. degree in English and journalism from New York University and a master's degree in library and information science from Pratt Institute.

Ms. Landau has worked as a newspaper reporter, a children's book editor, and a youth services librarian. She has written over thirty-five books for young people, including the biography *Robert Fulton* and *Black in America: A Fight For Freedom*, co-authored with Jesse Jackson.